Learning to Read & Think Book F

Thomas G. Gunning, Ed.D.

Professor, Reading Department
Southern Connecticut State University

Jamestown Publishers
Providence, Rhode Island

Learning to Read & Think Book F
Thomas G. Gunning, Ed.D.

Catalog No. 607
©1989 by Jamestown Publishers, Inc.

All rights reserved. The contents of this book are protected by the United States
Copyright Law. Address all inquiries to Editor, Jamestown Publishers,
Post Office Box 9168, Providence, Rhode Island 02940.

Cover and text design by Deborah Hulsey Christie

Color illustrations by Barbara Steadman

Cartoons by Rich Bishop

Printed in the United States FE

89 90 91 92 93 94 10 9 8 7 6 5 4 3 2 1

ISBN 0-89061-683-3

Books in the Series

Contents

About the Cover

The student on the cover
is striking the pose of
The Thinker. Because this
book teaches students to
think as they read, we felt
that Rodin's masterpiece
would make an appro-
priate subject to depict,
using students as models,
against a wall of books.

Auguste Rodin (1840–1917)
has been called the greatest
sculptor since Michelangelo. His
original *The Thinker* is currently on
display in Paris.

Rodin Museum, Philadelphia
Gift of Jules E. Mastbaum

To the Student

Have you ever been fooled by an ad in a newspaper or magazine or on the radio or TV? Have you ever sent away for a skateboard or a dress that looked wonderful in the ad but was not really that great? Maybe you even tried a new cereal because the advertisement promised it would taste great. But when you actually tried the cereal, you did not like the taste.

Everyone has been tricked by words at one time or another. The purpose of this book is to teach you how to judge the words you read and hear so that you will not be fooled by the information. *Learning to Read & Think* will explain the difference between a fact and an opinion. This book will teach you to recognize when words are used to appeal to your feelings rather than appeal to your mind. *Learning to Read & Think* will explain the difference between fair and unfair writing, and teach you how to use information to draw a logical conclusion. This book will also help you judge whether or not authors are experts about their subjects. *Learning to Read & Think* will help you judge whether or not authors present their ideas in fair or unfair ways.

Learning these skills does not mean that you will never be tricked by words again. But if you use the skills taught in *Learning to Read & Think,* you should not be fooled as often or as easily.

1 Understanding Facts and Opinions

Read the two sentences below. See if you can tell how they are different.

> More than 100 billion cards, letters, and packages are mailed each year.

> Writing letters is fun.

The first sentence is a factual statement. Factual statements can be proved either correct or incorrect. You can prove factual statements by counting, measuring, weighing, touching, hearing, or observing. The first sentence can be proved by counting all the cards, letters, and packages that are mailed in a year's time. If you add up all the numbers and they total more than 100 billion, then you have proved the statement to be correct. But suppose the total was only 99 billion, 999 million. Then you have proved the statement incorrect. The first sentence is still a factual statement. A statement does not have to be true or correct to be factual. You only have to be able to prove that it is right or wrong.

The second statement, "Writing letters is fun," is an opinion. An opinion is what you believe or how you feel about something. Some people enjoy writing letters, and others do not. Opinions cannot be proved. There is nothing about an opinion that can be counted, measured, weighed, touched, heard, or observed.

Read the following sentences. Write an **F** on the line if the sentence is a factual statement. Write an **O** if the sentence is an opinion statement. The first one has been done for you.

......**F**......   1. Bills and advertisements make up most of the mail delivered to homes.

....   2. Bills should be paid on time.

....   3. Advertisements are annoying.

....   4. The average adult buys about 30 greeting cards a year.

....   5. Many greeting cards are too expensive.

....   6. Thousands of letters cannot be delivered.

....   7. Many of those letters do not have full addresses.

....   8. People should be more careful when they address letters.

....   9. Letters that cannot be delivered are sent to the Dead Letter Office.

....   10. Recently the Dead Letter Office in Cincinnati, Ohio, delivered two sacks of mail sent in 1910 that had just been found in an old post office.

Read the selection and answer the questions that follow.

*W*hich house gets the most mail? It's probably the White House. Each day between 10,000 and 20,000 letters arrive at 1600 Pennsylvania Avenue. So much mail is sent to the White House that it takes more than a dozen people to open all the letters. Another 20 people spend their days reading the letters. Letters that ask questions are sent to people who have the special information that is requested. Letters that ask for help are sent to people who assist others. A few special letters are set aside for the president to read. Sometimes the president answers those letters personally. The president cannot possibly read all the letters that are addressed to him. But he is given a report of what people are saying in their letters. Ronald Reagan was a kind-hearted president. He frequently wrote personal replies to people who wrote to him. Sometimes he even telephoned the people.

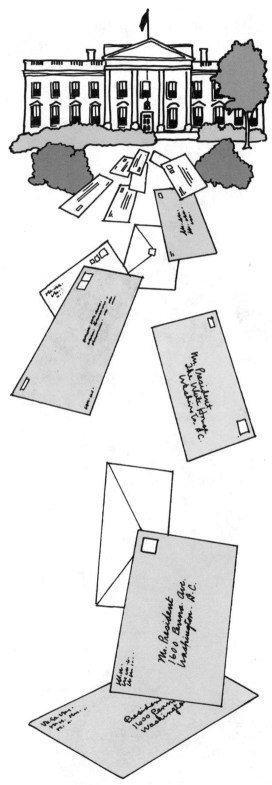

1. Which of the following statements is an opinion?
   ☐ a. Each day between 10,000 and 20,000 letters arrive at 1600 Pennsylvania Avenue.
   ☐ b. It takes more than a dozen people to open all the letters.
   ☐ c. Ronald Reagan was a kind-hearted president.

2. What are two opinions that you have about the mail or about letter writing? Write your opinions on the lines below.

   a. ....

   ....

   ....

   b. ....

   ....

   ....

Signal Words

Sometimes it is difficult to tell the difference between a fact and an opinion. There are words, however, that suggest that a statement may be an opinion. If a statement has adjectives like *good, better, best, excellent, fantastic, wonderful, marvelous, bad, worse, worst, awful, terrible,* or verbs like *believe, should, enjoy,* and *like,* then the statement is probably an opinion.

Read the following sentences. Write an **F** on the line if the sentence is a fact statement. Write an **O** if the sentence is an opinion statement. If the sentence is an opinion, underline any signal words in that sentence. The first one has been done for you.

O   1. Snakes are <u>fascinating</u> creatures.

.... 2. There are more than 2,600 different kinds of snakes.

.... 3. Only 210 of those snakes are poisonous.

.... 4. Poisonous snakes have hollow fangs.

.... 5. The poison goes through the snake's fangs into the snake's prey.

.... 6. One kind of snake has a poison that is so strong that just over one-thousandth of an ounce of the poison can kill 30,000 mice.

.... 7. Snakes are many different sizes.

.... 8. The king snake is one of the best snakes.

.... 9. The king snake eats mostly rats, mice, and poisonous snakes.

.... 10. The king snake is a wonderful creature.

.... 11. The black mamba is one of the worst snakes.

.... 12. The poisonous black mamba can strike quickly.

.... 13. The anaconda is the largest snake.

.... 14. A full-grown anaconda is 25 feet long.

.... 15. An anaconda can weigh about 250 pounds.

.... 16. Meeting an anaconda would be an awful experience.

.... 17. An anaconda can eat a 100-pound pig.

.... 18. The anaconda is an excellent hunter.

.... 19. The reticulated python is the longest snake.

.... 20. The reticulated python is a marvelous creature.

Read the selection and answer the questions that follow.

*T*he spitting cobra is a terrible snake. Spitting cobras have tiny openings in their fangs. They can spit their poison 10 or more feet away from themselves. These mean snakes aim for their victim's eyes. The cobras' deadly poison can blind their victims. Zookeepers who take care of spitting cobras wear special masks. Spitting cobras sometimes startle zoo visitors by spraying the glass cages with poison. It is an excellent idea to keep poisonous snakes in a glass cage. That way, no one gets hurt.

1. Which of the following statements is an opinion?
   ☐ a. The spitting cobra is a terrible snake.
   ☐ b. Spitting cobras have tiny openings in their fangs.
   ☐ c. Spitting cobras can spit poison 10 or more feet away from themselves.

2. Write down any words from the selection above that suggest opinions.

   ....

   ....

   ....

3. On the lines below, write three of your own opinions about snakes or other animals.

   a. ....

   ....

   ....

   b. ....

   ....

   ....

   c. ....

   ....

   ....

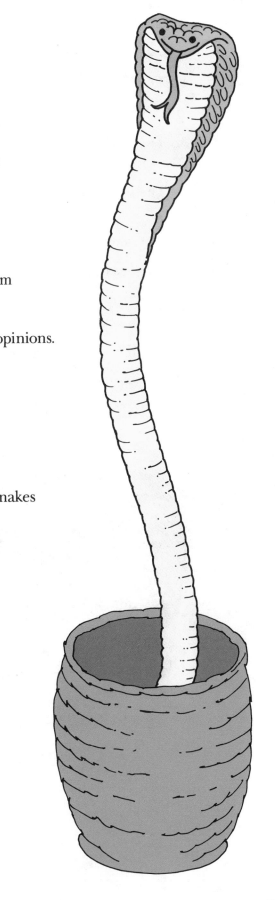

Read the following sentences. Write an **F** on the line if the
sentence is a factual statement. Write an **O** if the sentence is
an opinion statement.

...... F ...... 1. The largest flag ever made covered two acres.

.... 2. Two acres equals 9,680 square yards.

.... 3. The flag flew over a bridge in New York City
in 1976.

.... 4. The huge flag was a wonderful sight.

.... 5. The wind tore the flag to pieces in less than
an hour.

.... 6. Many of today's flags are made of nylon
or polyester.

.... 7. Nylon is lighter than polyester.

.... 8. Nylon flags look better than polyester flags do.

.... 9. Nylon costs more than polyester does.

.... 10. All flags should be made of nylon.

Read the following selection and answer the questions.

From 1892 to 1943 16 million newcomers stopped at Ellis Island. On Ellis Island immigrants were examined to see if they were healthy before they were allowed to settle in the United States. For most people, the exam was a frightening experience. If they failed the exam, they might be sent home. Two out of every 100 immigrants were sent home. Ellis Island was often overcrowded. Sometimes as many as 5,000 immigrants a day arrived on the island. The newcomers were often treated harshly. They were constantly ordered to move or to hurry. Most immigrants did not speak English. They were frightened when the workers shouted at them in a strange language. The workers at Ellis Island should have been kinder to the immigrants.

Which of the following statements is an opinion?
☐ a. From 1892 to 1943 16 million newcomers stopped at Ellis Island.
☐ b. The workers at Ellis Island should have been kinder to the immigrants.
☐ c. Two out of every 100 newcomers were sent home.

Checking Facts

Factual statements can be proved in a number of different ways. Some facts can be proved correct or incorrect by counting. Others can be proved by measuring, weighing, touching, listening, or observing. Some facts can be proved by checking an encyclopedia, a magazine, or a newspaper.

Read the factual statements below and note how each statement might be proved.

SENTENCE	PROOF
There are more than 35,000 different kinds of spiders.	Count
Orb weaver spiders spin round webs.	Observe
Dry threads are spun outward from the center of the web.	Touch
The orange garden spider's web is about two feet across.	Measure

Exercise A

Read the following factual statements about spiders. Then write on the line how you might prove each statement. You could use an encyclopedia or a book about spiders to prove each statement. But instead of saying "look in encyclopedia or book on spiders," tell whether you would mainly **count, measure, weigh, touch, listen,** or **observe** to prove each statement. Write only one word on each line. The first one has been done for you.

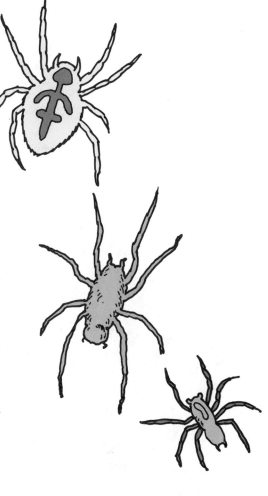

<u>observe</u>   1. Not all spiders can spin webs.

.... 2. Part of a spider's web is made of sticky silk.

.... 3. No two spider webs are exactly the same.

.... 4. Orb weaver spiders can rebuild their webs in about 30 minutes.

.... 5. One kind of spider can build a web that is nearly 50 feet across.

.... 6. About 300 thousand spiders live in a fifty-foot web.

.... 7. Each spider is about one-fifth of an inch long.

.... 8. The world's heaviest spider weighs more than four ounces.

.... 9. A spider's web vibrates when an insect is caught in it.

.... 10. Flies buzz louder than usual when they are caught in a web.

Read the stories and answer the questions.

STORY 1

*M*any strange planes have been built. Years ago an engineer named Zimmerman built a round plane. The plane was built but never flown. In 1958 an inflatable plane was constructed. The plane was easy to inflate. A vacuum cleaner was used to pump air into the plane. Because the plane was inflatable, it could land and float on the sea. Only 10 inflatable planes were ever built. The invention seemed more like a boat than a plane.

Which of the following statements is a fact?
- ☐ a. Many strange planes have been built.
- ☐ b. In 1958 an inflatable plane was constructed.
- ☐ c. The invention seemed more like a boat than a plane.

STORY 2

*I*n 1804 Lewis and Clark set out to explore the lands west of the Mississippi River. They wanted to find a route to the Pacific Ocean. Lewis and Clark hired Sacagawea and her husband, Charbonneau, to help them explore. Sacagawea, a Shoshone princess, acted as an interpreter. She explained to the native Americans what Lewis and Clark were saying. She let the explorers know what the native Americans were saying. Sacagawea was an excellent guide. She helped to guide the men through the rugged country. Sacagawea obtained food and horses for the explorers. Without the horses and food, they would not have been able to cross the Rocky Mountains. Sacagawea and Charbonneau stayed with Lewis and Clark until the explorers reached the Pacific Ocean. On the return trip, the two native Americans remained with the explorers all the way to North Dakota.

Which of the following statements is an opinion?
- ☐ a. Sacagawea, a Shoshone princess, acted as an interpreter.
- ☐ b. Sacagawea obtained food and horses for the explorers.
- ☐ c. Sacagawea was an excellent guide.

Read the stories and answer the questions.

STORY 1

A millionaire named Lang returned to his elementary school a few years ago. He was going to give the 61 sixth-graders some tips on becoming a success. Halfway through his speech, Lang decided that he wanted to give the students something more than just words. He said that he would give them all a college education if they worked hard in school. If their families did not have the money, he promised to pay their way through college. Eugene Lang is a generous man.

Mr. Lang contributed more than money to the sixth-grade class. He arranged for tutors to help the students study, and he planned visits to colleges. He also met with the students frequently and offered them advice and encouragement. Most of the students accepted Mr. Lang's offer and went to college. Mr. Lang's idea spread throughout the country. Hundreds of other wealthy people have paid for the college educations of thousands of youngsters.

Which of the following statements is an opinion?
- ☐ a. Eugene Lang is a generous man.
- ☐ b. There were 61 sixth-graders in the elementary school.
- ☐ c. Most of the students accepted Mr. Lang's offer.

STORY 2

*P*eople did not believe that Alice Stebbins Wells was a police officer for the city of Los Angeles. In 1910 police officers were allowed to ride Los Angeles's trolleys and streetcars without paying a fare. When Wells showed the conductor her badge, the conductor demanded that she pay. "That's your husband's badge," the conductor said. Wells solved the problem by requesting a special badge that said "Policewoman's Badge No. 1." Wells was one of the country's first policewomen. She was an excellent officer.

Which of the following statements is an opinion?
- ☐ a. In 1910 police officers were allowed to ride Los Angeles's trolleys and streetcars without paying a fare.
- ☐ b. Wells was one of the country's first policewomen.
- ☐ c. Wells was an excellent officer.

4

Analyzing Facts

How would you prove the following sentences?

A dime is worth ten cents.

A groundhog is a woodchuck.

The sentences above cannot be proved by counting, measuring, weighing, touching, listening, or observing. The sentences can only be proved by knowing what all the words mean and seeing if the sentences make sense. You do not have to look at a groundhog and a woodchuck to see if they are the same animal. If you look in the dictionary, you will see that *groundhog* and *woodchuck* are two different names for the same animal. You do not have to count ten pennies to know that a dime is worth ten cents. The word *dime* means ten cents. This special kind of factual sentence is called an analytical statement. You can prove it to be correct or incorrect by analyzing the statement, or looking closely at its parts.

Read the following factual sentences. Then write on the line how you might prove each statement. Write only one word on each line. Tell whether you would mainly **count**, **measure**, **weigh**, **touch**, **listen**, **observe**, or **analyze** statements. Look up in a dictionary any words that you do not know. The first one has been done for you.

analyze   1. A triangle has three sides.

....   2. The new house is shaped like a triangle.

....   3. A pentagon has five sides.

....   4. A dozen means twelve.

....   5. Alicia has a dozen pets.

....   6. The blue whale is a huge animal.

....   7. A blue whale may be as long as a line of 30 cars.

....   8. A trillion is 1,000 billion or 1,000,000,000,000

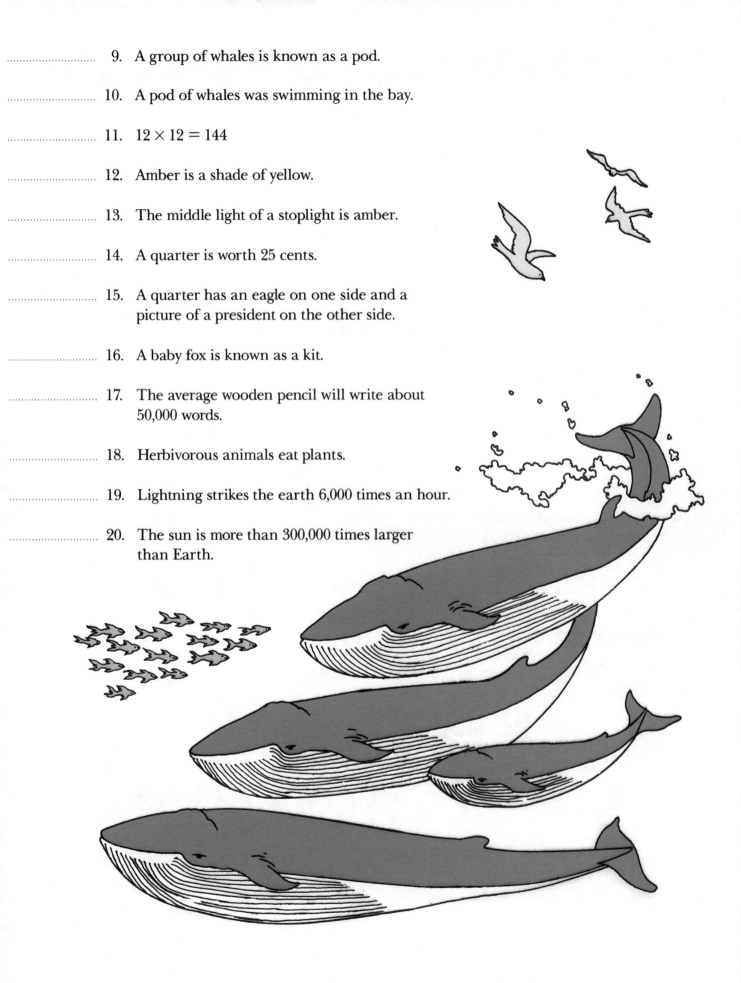

.... 9. A group of whales is known as a pod.

.... 10. A pod of whales was swimming in the bay.

.... 11. $12 \times 12 = 144$

.... 12. Amber is a shade of yellow.

.... 13. The middle light of a stoplight is amber.

.... 14. A quarter is worth 25 cents.

.... 15. A quarter has an eagle on one side and a picture of a president on the other side.

.... 16. A baby fox is known as a kit.

.... 17. The average wooden pencil will write about 50,000 words.

.... 18. Herbivorous animals eat plants.

.... 19. Lightning strikes the earth 6,000 times an hour.

.... 20. The sun is more than 300,000 times larger than Earth.

Unit One Review

Read the following questions and write your answers on the lines.

1. What is an opinion?

....

....

2. What is a fact?

....

....

3. What are some ways in which facts can be proved?

....

....

4. How are analytical statements proved?

....

....

5. Give an example of an analytical statement.

....

....

6. Locate three interesting facts in a library or school book. Write the facts and tell how each might be proved.

   a. ....

   b. ....

   c. ....

7. Locate three opinions in a library or school book. Write the opinions on the lines below.

   a. ....

   b. ....

   c. ....

UNIT TWO

1 What Words Communicate

The words *Richard*, *woman*, *Idaho*, *kitchen*, *jet*, and *radio* name persons, places, and things. Words like *shout*, *hum*, *skip*, *chuckle*, and *drop* name actions. Some words do more than just name. They judge or give an opinion. Compare the two sentences below. See if you can tell which sentence simply describes an action and which judges the action.

> Robert picked up the money.
>
> Robert stole the money.

The first sentence simply describes an action. It tells you that Robert picked up some money. The second sentence judges what Robert did. It says that Robert did something dishonest: he stole some money.

Always be aware that words can judge an action. Words that judge are frequently used by people who want you to agree with their ideas or to buy something that people are selling.

THE SENATOR OBVIOUSLY STOLE THE ELECTION AND...

CHANNEL 13 OPINION NEWS

Read the following sentences. Circle **describes** or **judges** to show how the underlined word or words are used. The first two sentences have been done for you.

1. Janice is my <u>neighbor</u>.

   (describes) judges

2. I just finished a <u>500-page</u> book.

   (describes) judges

3. Janice is a <u>pest</u>.

   describes   judges

4. There goes <u>Jed Franklin</u>.

   describes   judges

5. I just finished an <u>exciting</u> book.

   describes   judges

6. There goes the <u>criminal</u>.

   describes   judges

7. That dog is a <u>collie</u>.

   describes   judges

8. That dog is a <u>monster</u>.

   describes   judges

9. We <u>enjoyed</u> the movie.

   describes   judges

10. The hyena is a <u>swift</u> animal.

  describes   judges

11. The hyena is a <u>cowardly</u> animal.

  describes   judges

12. Ruth <u>bragged about</u> her trip.

  describes   judges

13. Temperatures reached <u>102</u> degrees.

  describes   judges

14. It was a <u>miserable</u> day.

  describes   judges

15. Carmen <u>teased</u> her brother.

  describes   judges

Exercise B

Finish each of the following sentences with a word or a group of words that judge.

1. Wrestling is ....

2. Broccoli is ....

3. Mornings are ....

4. Puppies are ....

5. TV is ....

2 How Descriptions Sound

At yesterday's baseball game, your friend Maria said she got four hits. She said she saved the game by leaping high into the air to make an unbelievable catch. You were there. Maria got one hit and struck out three times. Maria made her unbelievable catch when she waved with her gloved hand to Anne, who was sitting in the stands. The ball landed right in the middle of Maria's glove. Maria did not have to move an inch. The catch was an accident. You tell Maria that she is *lying*. When she realizes that you were at the game, Maria admits that she may have been *exaggerating*.

Lying and *exaggerating* both describe the same action, but *exaggerating* sounds much better than *lying* does. Words can often be chosen to make an action, a person, a place, or a thing sound better. Always notice when words are used in this way. They are sometimes chosen to hide the truth.

Cathy had the lead part in the school play. She tells you how well she acted her part, how the audience applauded, and how she was much better than everyone else. You tell her she is *bragging*. She says she is simply *describing* what happened. The word *bragging* makes the action sound worse than the word *describing* does. Words can be chosen to make an action sound better. They can also be chosen to make an action sound worse.

In the sentences below, circle the word or words that make the action, person, or thing sound **better**. The first sentence has been done for you.

1. Our team was (defeated / wiped out) in a nine-inning game.

2. The game was (boring / slow-moving).

3. The players made several (careless / stupid) plays.

4. The coach (bawled out / corrected) the players after the game.

5. The hot dogs at the game were (undercooked / raw).

6. The hamburgers were (greasy / juicy).

7. Anna is (sloppy / disorganized).

8. Anna (forgot / neglected) her chores.

9. Anna's grandparents live in a (quaint / weird) house.

10. Anna's grandparents are (ancient / mature).

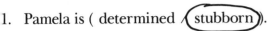
n the sentences below, circle the word or words that make the
ction, person, place, or thing sound **worse**. The first sentence
as been done for you.

1. Pamela is (determined / (stubborn)).

2. She (always wants her own way / is independent).

3. Pamela usually (convinces / orders) other people to do
   what she wants them to do.

4. Pamela becomes (furious / irritated) when no one
   listens to her.

5. The trip down the river was (adventurous / foolhardy).

6. That horse is (bony / thin).

7. Pigs eat (garbage / leftovers).

8. The boring speech was (endless / long).

9. José (pestered / asked) until his father finally agreed.

0. "I have too much work to do," Fred (commented / moaned).

Words That Sell

3

Words are often used to persuade. A candy bar may be described as "chock full of crunchy peanuts and chewy caramel and covered with a thick coat of rich, mouth-watering chocolate." After they read such a description, some people are ready to hurry to the closest store and buy that brand of candy bar. Words like *crunchy, chewy,* and *mouth-watering* help people to imagine what the candy bar will taste like. Those words make the candy sound delicious.

Advertisers use words like *new, improved, extra, adventure, excitement, value,* and *quality* because they help to sell products. People like products that are new and improved or that promise fun, adventure, and excitement.

Read the ads below. Underline the words that are used to persuade or to make the food sound really good.

1 Golden Ripe
Honeydew Melons
$**1.49** each

2 Mouth-watering, Super-Jumbo
Cantaloupe
$**1.09** each

3 Crunchy
Cucumbers
59¢ lb.

4 Farm-Fresh,
Golden Corn
4 ears $ **1**

5 Tender, Delicious
Grapes
$**1.29** lb.

6 Large, Luscious
Plums
89¢ lb.

Read the following ads. Underline the words that are used to persuade.

1

What has more power than GLEAMO?

New, improved **GLEAMO** now has extra cleaning power.

New, improved **GLEAMO** is better than ever.

2

Experience the excitement of some of the greatest moments in sports.

Visit the SPORTS HALL OF FAME

Put some fun into your life.

3

We don't build bikes.
We build excitement.
TALL TIMBER TRAIL BIKES
will take you anywhere you want to go.

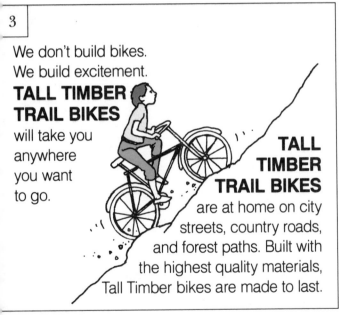

TALL TIMBER TRAIL BIKES are at home on city streets, country roads, and forest paths. Built with the highest quality materials, Tall Timber bikes are made to last.

4

When you buy clothing at
MARTHA'S,
you know you're getting the best.

Quality is our middle name.

Stop in today for a look at our back-to-school fashions.

5

Shop at
Franklin's Discount Department Store.

We have extra values and extra savings in every department.

We know how to stretch your dollar.

Unit Two Review

Read the following questions and write your answers on the lines.

1. What are three important ways in which words can be used?

   ....

   ....

   ....

2. Listen to three ads on the radio or TV or read three ads in a newspaper or magazine. Write down all the words in the ads that are used to persuade.

   Ad 1: ....

   ....

   ....

   ....

   Ad 2: ....

   ....

   ....

   ....

   Ad 3: ....

   ....

   ....

   ....

UNIT THREE

Fair and Unfair Writing

Read the following three stories. One story is fair; one story is slanted against sailors; one story is slanted for sailors. See if you can tell which story is which.

STORY 1

In 1741 a Russian ship sailed near a large group of magnificent sea animals in the Bering Sea. The animals became known as Steller's sea cows. The sea cows were 25 feet long and weighed close to 10,000 pounds. Hungry for fresh meat, the sailors murdered one of the large, trusting cows. The heartless crews of other sailing and whaling ships did the same. At the time they were first discovered, there were about 5,000 of these special sea cows. But by 1768 the Steller's sea cow was extinct. Greedy sailors had cruelly slaughtered these poor defenseless animals.

STORY 2

In 1741 courageous sailors braving the cold waters of the Bering Sea noticed some very large, stupid animals. The animals became known as Steller's sea cows. Starved for fresh meat, the sailors had no choice but to eat one of the useless beasts. Other sailors did the same. In 1741 there were a few Steller's sea cows around. By 1768 there were no more left.

STORY 3

In 1741 a group of Russian sailors discovered a large sea creature which became known as Steller's sea cow. The sailors had not had fresh meat for a long time. They ate one of the creatures. The crews of other ships sailing in that area also ate sea cows. Unfortunately, the sailors killed too many of the sea cows. By 1768 Steller's sea cow was extinct.

Story 3 is fair. It simply states the facts. Story 1 states the same facts, but Story 1 uses words that make the sailors sound bad and the sea cows sound good. Words like *murdered, slaughtered, heartless,* and *greedy* turn readers against the sailors. The story uses words like *magnificent, trusting,* and *defenseless* to make readers admire and feel sorry for Steller's sea cows.

Story 2, on the other hand, is slanted in favor of the sailors. It uses words like *courageous, braving,* and *starved* to make sailors sound good, but it uses words like *stupid, useless,* and *beasts* to turn readers against the sea cows.

Writers can choose details that make a person, place, thing, or idea sound really good or really bad. Slanted writing unfairly uses both words and details to make a person, place, thing, or idea sound better or worse than it really is.

Read the following stories about the circus. Look for words and details that slant the articles. Then answer the questions that follow.

STORY 1

*B*eing in a circus can be tiresome. Circus performers spend much of their lives traveling from one city to another. Soon the cities begin to look alike and traveling becomes boring. When they arrive at a new city, the performers must unpack. Then they must search for a grocery store that may be blocks or even miles away. Often they are bothered by nosy strangers who ask them many dull questions, such as, What is circus life like? Isn't it exciting moving from town to town? During the show, the performers wait nervously in tiny, crowded dressing rooms.

STORY 2

*B*eing in a circus is fun. Circus performers don't have to stay in one dull town. They spend much of their lives traveling from one exciting city to another. When they arrive in a new town, the performers unpack. Then the circus performers are free to explore their new home. They meet interesting people and visit the city's famous sights. During the shows, the performers feel happy when their acts are announced and the crowd cheers and applauds.

1. Which story, 1 or 2, is slanted in favor of the circus?

    ....

2. From the story slanted in favor of the circus, what are some words that make working in the circus sound good?

    ....

    ....

3. From the story slanted against the circus, what are some words that make working in the circus sound bad?

    ....

    ....

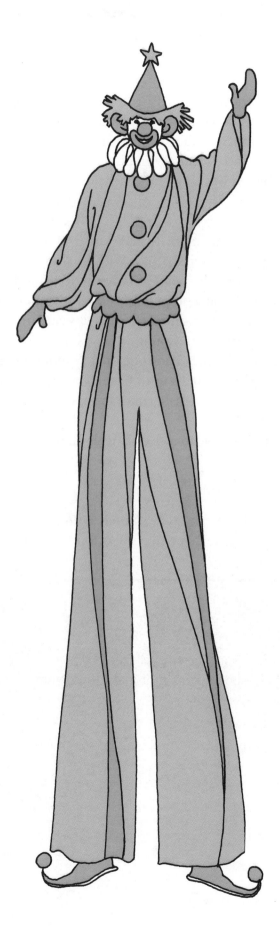

Read the stories and answer the questions.

STORY 1

*I*n the spring of 1935, a fisherman stepped on a large octopus. Not knowing what had attacked it, the poor frightened animal grabbed onto the man who had stepped on it. The octopus, by instinct, began swimming out to sea. Just then, another man began hacking at the helpless creature with a knife.

STORY 2

*I*n the spring of 1935, Frank Count was attacked while fishing in San Francisco Bay. With its slimy tentacles, an evil octopus grabbed the helpless fisherman around the body, legs, and left arm. Unable to pull away from the monster, Frank yelled for help. Harry Simmons, who was catching fish nearby, hurried to help Frank Count, who was being pulled out into deep water by the vicious octopus. Simmons cut off several of the creature's arms until Count was free. Simmons then helped the terrified fisherman to shore.

1. Which story, 1 or 2, is slanted against the octopus?

    ....

2. From the story slanted against the octopus, what are some words that make the octopus sound bad?

    ....

    ....

3. From the story slanted in favor of the octopus, what are some words that make the octopus sound good?

    ....

    ....

Exercise C

Read the stories and answer the questions.

STORY 1

*F*eral animals are tame or domesticated animals that live on their own. They have become wild again. Small bands of feral goats are found in 27 of the 50 states. Feral horses and burros are found in many western states. Feral pigs roam several southern states and Hawaii. Feral dogs and cats are found in nearly every city and town and in many farm areas.

STORY 2

*F*eral pigs are a menace. They will eat anything. Wild pigs in Hawaii gobble up berries, seeds, grasses, and farmers' crops. The greedy wild pigs also eat other animals. Feral pigs eat frogs, earthworms, and birds' eggs. Feral pigs destroy creatures that are helpful to people. Feral pigs often trample young plants in fields, destroy orchards, and drink up water that belongs to cows and sheep. Vicious feral pigs have also attacked horses, dogs, and people.

STORY 3

*F*eral pigs like to eat. Often they eat harmful insects and animals. Helpful feral pigs eat thousands of grasshoppers, mice, and rats. Kindly feral pigs save birds' eggs by eating snakes that destroy eggs. As they root in the ground for food, feral pigs loosen the soil. Some crops grow faster and better after hardworking feral pigs have rooted in a field. Although they may attack dogs that are chasing them, feral pigs don't usually bother people. The pigs generally run away when people are around.

1. Which story—1, 2, or 3—is the fairest?

....

2. Which story—1, 2, or 3—is slanted against feral pigs?

....

3. From the story slanted against feral pigs, what are some words that make the pigs sound bad?

....

....

4. From the story slanted in favor of feral pigs, what are some words that make the pigs sound good?

....

....

Read the stories and answer the questions.

STORY 1

*I*n 1975 there was a fad known as the pet rock. More than a million people paid $4 to buy a small rock that was packaged in a cardboard box. Packed with the pet rock was a small booklet that told people how to train the rock. For example, to teach a pet rock how to roll over, all you had to do was to place the rock on a steep hill.

STORY 2

*P*et rocks were a brilliant idea. Pet rocks were cute to look at and fun to have, but they didn't bark, bite, chase cars, or get fleas. They didn't need to be washed, fed, or taken to the vet for shots. Pet rocks were inexpensive. They cost only $4. That price included a handy cardboard carrying case and a clever instruction booklet. No wonder smart buyers bought more than a million pet rocks in just a few months. Pet rocks were the perfect pet.

STORY 3

*P*et rocks were one of the worst fads of all time. More than a million people stupidly paid $4 for an ugly rock in a cheap cardboard box. The foolish buyers said they had the perfect pet because it didn't bite, bark, or chase cars. In truth, the rock didn't do anything at all. It didn't purr, wag its tail, or greet its owner. What a boring pet! What a stupid idea!

1. Which story—1, 2, or 3—is the fairest?

   ....

2. Which story—1, 2, or 3—is slanted against pet rocks?

   ....

3. From the story slanted against pet rocks, what are some words that make the idea of pet rocks sound bad?

   ....

   ....

4. From the story slanted in favor of pet rocks, what are some words that make the idea of pet rocks sound good?

   ....

   ....

Unit Three Review

Read the following questions and write your answers on the lines.

1. What is slanted writing?

   ....

   ....

2. What are some words that might be used to slant writing in favor of a person, place, or thing?

   ....

   ....

3. What are some words that might be used to slant writing against a person, place, or thing?

   ....

   ....

4. In a newspaper, magazine, library book, or school book, find two examples of slanted writing: one that is slanted for something and one that is slanted against something.

   Slanted For

   ....

   ....

   ....

   ....

   ....

   Slanted Against

   ....

   ....

   ....

   ....

   ....

UNIT FOUR

Recognizing the Author's Purpose

Read the following paragraphs. See if you can discover why each paragraph was written.

PARAGRAPH 1

One of the best-tasting fish in the world is also one of the largest. The arapaima may grow to be 15 feet long and weigh over 300 pounds. This huge fish lives in the Amazon River, the world's largest river. Unfortunately, the arapaima may be in danger of dying out. Since arapaima taste so good and bring such a high price, they are often caught by fishermen.

PARAGRAPH 2

The arapaima is being overfished. Years ago, only full-grown arapaima were harpooned by fishermen. Now, with the widespread use of nets, both full-grown and baby arapaima are being caught. Because of this wasteful way of fishing, the arapaima will soon die out. Isn't it time that we go back to harpooning as a method of catching arapaima? Let's stop using nets and give this endangered animal a chance to survive.

PARAGRAPH 3

Their food had run out weeks ago. The lost explorers had trapped a few small animals, but that wasn't nearly enough food for the 20 members of the group. Suddenly Carmen saw a giant fish heave itself up out of the water and gulp down a mouthful of air. It was an arapaima, the delicious, air-breathing fish that she had read about but never had seen. Carmen wondered how she could catch the giant fish. Quickly, she grabbed the boat's landing lines and fashioned a large lasso. "There's more than one way to catch a fish," Carmen thought to herself.

All three paragraphs are about arapaima. Each paragraph was written for a different reason or purpose. Paragraph 1 was written to give information. For example, it tells you how large the arapaima is and where it is found. The author wrote Paragraph 1 to inform. School books, encyclopedias, nonfiction books, and articles in newspapers and magazines are written to inform.

Paragraph 2 was written to persuade. The author is trying to persuade fishermen to stop using nets so that the arapaima will not die out. The author presents some factual information in Paragraph 2, but his or her main purpose for writing the paragraph is to convince people to use harpoons instead of nets. Advertisements, letters to the editor, editorials in newspapers, and ads on TV are created to persuade.

Paragraph 3 tells about Carmen, a fictional character who decides to lasso an arapaima. Paragraph 3 was written to bring enjoyment to the reader. Its purpose is to entertain.

It is important to be able to identify the author's purpose. A person who is trying to persuade may give information but may leave out important facts. For example, the author of Paragraph 2 says that the arapaima is in danger of dying out because both full-grown and baby arapaima are caught in nets. The paragraph does not mention that there is a law saying that arapaima under four feet long must be thrown back. Paragraph 2 does not tell you that many poor fishermen need to sell arapaima so they will have money to buy food and clothing for their families. If readers knew those facts, they might disagree with the writer's request that fishermen stop using nets.

Read the following paragraphs. Decide whether each paragraph has been written mainly to inform, to entertain, or to persuade. Write **I** (Inform), **P** (Persuade), or **E** (Entertain) on the line next to each paragraph.

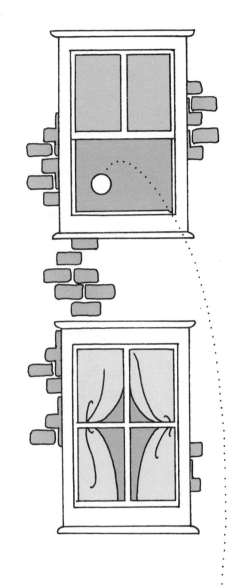

.... 1.   People usually feel safer when they swim in lakes. After all, sharks live in the ocean. But there is one lake where sharks have been living for thousands of years. Lake Nicaragua is the home of the Lake Nicaragua shark, a fierce animal that has attacked a number of humans. How did this shark get into the lake? No one really knows. Scientists believe that there was once a waterway flowing between Lake Nicaragua and the Caribbean Sea.

.... 2.   The building's brick wall looked like a good place for Bill to practice his backhand. A shot off the edge of his racquet sent the tennis ball through an upper-story window. As he raced up the rickety stairs, Bill crashed through a rotted step. He didn't break any bones, but no matter how hard he tried, he couldn't pull his legs free. There was no use calling for help. No one would hear him. What could he do?

.... 3.   Have you ever wondered how young TV and movie stars get their schooling? Some can go to regular schools, but others must travel from city to city. Young actors who travel have tutors who travel with them. Some actors go to special schools like the Professional Children's School in New York City. When they have to be on the road, the young performers take their assignments with them. They mail their completed homework back to their teachers, and their teachers mail them new lessons and new assignments.

4. Want to make a big hit with your baseball team? Try Practice Bat. With Practice Bat, you can practice hitting in the privacy of your own backyard. With a Practice Bat, you swing at a ray of light. When you hit the ray, you hear a cheering sound. When you miss, Practice Bat is programmed to tell you what you did wrong. Be a great hitter. Try Practice Bat.

5. For Kim, it was a dream come true. If she sang well tonight, she might be offered a record or a movie contract. She nervously crossed the stage to the microphone. A thunder of applause greeted her. The band started playing her first number. Kim picked up the microphone. She opened her mouth and started to sing, but no sound came out—not even a squeak.

6. Frighten your friends with an inflatable shark. It looks so real that your friends will race out of the water. The shark is made of genuine plastic. It can be hung in your room . . . if you're brave enough.

7. Alexander Fleming was a scientist who studied germs. After accidentally leaving a dish of germs uncovered, he discovered that some of the germs had been destroyed by a mold. This accident led to the discovery of penicillin, one of the most important medicines of all time.

8. Do you want to make some spending money? Buy a Speedy Button Maker. With a Speedy Button Maker, you can make dozens of different kinds of buttons. Put any name, saying, or photo on your custom-made buttons. Sell your buttons at schools, at games, and at fairs. With a Speedy Button Maker, you'll never be short of cash or buttons again. Speedy Button Makers cost just $29.95.

Read the stories and answer the questions.

STORY 1

*H*ow do people who are both deaf and blind communicate with others? They make special signs on the hand of another person. Now, with the help of a robot named Dexter, people who are both deaf and blind can receive phone messages. On a computer hooked up to a phone line, a person types out a message. The message travels over the phone line and activates the receiving computer. The message is then spelled out by Dexter, who is attached to the receiving computer. The deaf-blind person puts his or her hand under the robot's fingers. In that way, the person gets the message.

1. What is the author's main purpose?
   - ☐ a. to convince people to buy Dexter
   - ☐ b. to tell a story that has a robot as a main character
   - ☐ c. to tell how a robot can help people who are both deaf and blind

2. In the story the author is trying to
   - ☐ a. inform.
   - ☐ b. entertain.
   - ☐ c. persuade.

STORY 2

*J*ust before sunset, as Jessie packed up her fishing pole, a large tanker truck backed up to the lake. The driver jumped out of the truck, looked around, quickly hooked up a hose, and turned a large valve. A milky liquid began pouring into the lake. The liquid made a hissing sound as it hit the lake's clear water.

3. What is the author's main purpose?
   - ☐ a. to persuade people to keep our waterways clean
   - ☐ b. to explain how lakes become polluted
   - ☐ c. to tell the beginning of a story

4. In this selection the author is trying to
   - ☐ a. inform.
   - ☐ b. entertain.
   - ☐ c. persuade.

Read the stories and answer the questions.

STORY 1

Cars of the future may be powered by the sun. Not long ago, a solar-powered car known as the Sunraycer drove over 2,000 miles of Australia's toughest roads in just 5½ days. The Sunraycer looks like a spaceship with fish scales. In those fish scales are 7,200 solar cells. The cells change the sun's energy into electricity which drives the car's tiny but powerful eight-pound motor. Rounded and sleek, the Sunraycer cuts easily through the wind and coasts along at speeds of about 40 miles an hour. You'll probably never see the Sunraycer on a highway, but within a few years you may see solar cars that use ideas first tried out on the Sunraycer.

1. What is the author's purpose?
   ☐ a. to tell an adventure story
   ☐ b. to persuade people to buy solar-powered cars
   ☐ c. to tell about a solar-powered car

2. In this story the author is trying to
   ☐ a. inform.
   ☐ b. entertain.
   ☐ c. persuade.

STORY 2

You sit down on the sand and turn on your radio. After only a few songs the radio begins to fade. Then it stops completely. The batteries are dead. What you need is a Sunsong radio. You'll never have to worry about dead batteries again. Sunsong uses solar cells for power. Brighten up your life with a Sunsong radio. A Sunsong may cost a little more, but with a Sunsong, you'll never have to buy another battery.

3. What is the author's main purpose?
   ☐ a. to tell a story about a day at the beach
   ☐ b. to convince people to buy a Sunsong radio
   ☐ c. to explain the advantages of a solar-powered radio

4. In this story the author is trying to
   ☐ a. inform.
   ☐ b. entertain.
   ☐ c. persuade.

Read the stories and answer the questions.

STORY 1

*T*he creatures were so strange. They ran around on a large striped field kicking a round object. "What had the object done to them?" Kay Seven wondered. A bell rang and the creatures ran into a long flat box. For the rest of the afternoon the group that had been kicking the round object sat hunched over some papers. The members of the group were making marks on the papers with small sticks. Another bell rang and the creatures hurried out of the large flat box and got into yellow boxes with wheels. The yellow boxes rolled away. "What strange creatures these Earthlings are!" Kay Seven commented to herself.

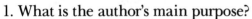

1. What is the author's main purpose?
   ☐ a. to tell an interesting story about a creature from space
   ☐ b. to persuade students to work harder at school
   ☐ c. to explain what schools are like

2. The author is trying to
   ☐ a. inform.
   ☐ b. entertain.
   ☐ c. persuade.

STORY 2

*L*ife was difficult for children in colonial times. There wasn't much time for play. Children helped around the house or farm as soon as they were old enough. Girls spent much of their time sewing, cooking, and making cloth. Boys were busy with either farm chores or with learning carpentry, shoemaking, or a similar trade. Children were expected to be respectful and obedient. There wasn't much time for play. When they did have free time, the children played tag, leapfrog, checkers, or played with homemade toys. Children became ill more often in the 1600s and 1700s. There were fewer medicines in those days, and doctors knew less about healing the sick. One child out of every three died before reaching the age of ten.

3. What is the author's main purpose?
   ☐ a. to give information about colonial times
   ☐ b. to persuade today's children that life is easy for them
   ☐ c. to tell a story that took place many years ago

4. The author is mainly trying to
   ☐ a. inform.
   ☐ b. entertain.
   ☐ c. persuade.

Read the stories and answer the questions.

STORY 1

Gardeners grow more tomatoes than they grow any other fruit. People like tomatoes, and tomatoes are easy to grow. Tomatoes are also excellent sources of vitamins A and C. At one time, however, many people were afraid to eat tomatoes. Tomatoes were said to be poisonous. Colonel Robert Gibbon Johnson knew that tomatoes were not poisonous. On a warm summer day in 1820, he stood on the steps of the Salem, New Jersey, courthouse and ate not one, but a whole basketful of ripe red tomatoes. The crowd was shocked. They waited for the colonel to collapse and become deathly ill, but nothing happened. The colonel proved that tomatoes are a harmless food. Thanks to the colonel, tomatoes became a favorite food. New Jersey later became one of the largest growers of tomatoes.

STORY 2

Tired of dry sandwiches for lunch? Try a steaming hot bowl of tasty Wonder Tomato Soup. Wonder Tomato Soup is made from fresh, juicy tomatoes grown on our own farms. Wonder Tomato Soup is full of vitamins A and C. Delicious Wonder Tomato Soup builds strong bones and healthy skin and teeth. For a wonderful meal, treat yourself to a bowl of Wonder Tomato Soup.

1. Which story was written mainly to persuade?

   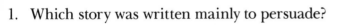
   ....

2. What was the author trying to persuade readers to do?

   ....

3. What was the purpose of the other story?

   ....

Read the stories and answer the questions.

STORY 1

*B*reakfast is a more popular meal than it used to be. Fewer people are skipping breakfast. A few years ago, 5 out of every 100 people skipped breakfast. Now that number is down to 4 out of 100. Scientists say that breakfast is an important meal, especially for students. The right kind of breakfast helps keep the mind alert. Students who eat breakfast tend to do better work than those who don't eat breakfast.

STORY 2

*W*ant to do better in school? Eat a better breakfast. Scientific studies show that students who eat breakfast do better in school than those who don't eat breakfast. Good Morning Frozen Breakfast features delicious meals that can be prepared in just two minutes in a microwave oven. Start your morning with Good Morning and watch those Cs turn into Bs and As.

1. Which story was written mainly to inform?

   ....

2. What was the purpose of the other story?

   ....

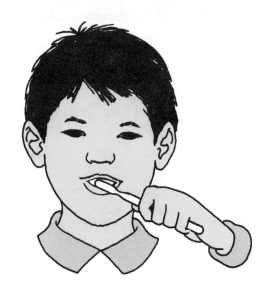

Exercise G

Read the stories and answer the questions.

STORY 1

There's good news for young people. Fewer children are getting cavities. In the early 1970s nearly three children out of every four had a cavity or two by the time they were ten. By the late 1970s, that number was cut to two out of three children. In the late 1980s, almost half the children under ten had no cavities. Older children also had fewer cavities. Why are there fewer cavities these days? Fluoride seems to be the main reason. Fluoride helps cut down on tooth decay by stopping the growth of harmful germs. Fluoride is found naturally in some drinking water and is added to drinking water in many cities and towns. Fluoride is also put in some toothpastes.

STORY 2

Cut down on cavities. New, improved Power toothpaste now contains fluoride. Scientific studies show that people who brush with a toothpaste that contains fluoride have fewer cavities than those who don't use fluoride. Power also freshens your breath as it cleans your teeth. New, improved Power comes in handy pump dispensers.

1. Which story was written to persuade?

   ....

2. What was the author trying to persuade readers to do?

   ....

3. What was the purpose of the other story?

   ....

Unit Four Review

Read the following questions and write your answers on the lines.

1. What are the three main purposes for writing?

   a. ....

   b. ....

   c. ....

2. What is the main purpose for writing each of the following?

   a. .... a humorous play

   b. .... an explanation of how computers work

   c. .... an ad for computers

   d. .... a story about a boy who has a talking dog

   e. .... a book about a famous explorer

3. In the library find a book that matches each of the three main purposes for writing. Write the title of each book and its purpose on the lines below.

   Title ....

   Purpose ....

   ....

   Title ....

   Purpose ....

   ....

   Title ....

   Purpose ....

   ....

1

Drawing Logical Conclusions

To draw a conclusion, you must think like a judge. You consider all the evidence before you make up your mind. When you read, you think about all the information. Then you come to a conclusion. A conclusion is an idea that is based on all the facts and details that you read.

Read the following article about baseball. Carefully think about the facts. Come to a conclusion about who invented baseball. Then answer the questions that follow the article.

Baseball is one of the most popular sports in the United States. For a while, people thought that Abner Doubleday invented baseball in 1839 in Cooperstown, New York. Doubleday's game had bases, fielders, and a batter. In Doubleday's game, however, players put runners out by hitting them with a ball. This was the way a game called rounders was played. Rounders was a game that had been popular in England since the 1700s. It had been brought to the United States by the colonists.

In 1845 a man named Alexander Cartwright drew up a list of rules for baseball. In Cartwright's rules a player was tagged instead of being hit with the ball. There were nine players on a team and three outs in an inning. These rules are still in effect today, but some older rules, such as having 21 aces, or innings, have been changed.

Cartwright got many of his ideas for rules from a book written by Robin Carver, an American writer. Carver, in turn, got some of his ideas from an English book called *The Boy's Own Book.*

Which of the following sentences is the best conclusion for this article?
☐ a. Abner Doubleday invented baseball.
☐ b. Alexander Cartwright invented baseball.
☐ c. Several people deserve credit for the invention of baseball.

The best answer is *c.* Doubleday's game was similar to rounders, a game brought from England. Cartwright made up rules for baseball, but some of those rules were borrowed from a book by Robin Carver. When you combine all this information, you can see that several people deserve credit for the invention of baseball.

Read the selection and answer the questions that follow.

The Model T Ford wasn't much to look at. Its square passenger compartment made it look like a box on wheels. Many people joked about its color. "You can get any color Model T you want," people used to say, "as long as it's black." Between 1908 and 1927, more than 15 million Model Ts were sold. The cars were easy to drive, didn't break down very often, and were simple to repair. Above all, the cars were cheap. The price of the Model T changed over the years. The price fell from $850 in 1908 to just $290 in 1926.

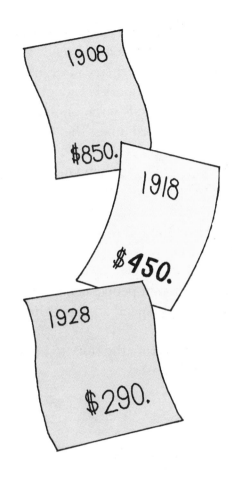

1. Which of the following sentences is the best conclusion for this selection?
   ☐ a. The Model T looked like a sports car.
   ☐ b. The Model T was a luxury car.
   ☐ c. The Model T was cheap and practical.

2. List details from the selection to help support the conclusion you have chosen.

....

....

....

....

Read the stories and answer the questions that follow.

STORY 1

*H*ow much sleep do people need? People need enough sleep so that they feel rested and ready for a day of school, work, or fun. Some adults feel fine after just three or four hours of sleep. Five or six hours is enough sleep for many people. The average adult needs seven or eight hours. A number of adults, however, feel tired unless they get nine or ten hours of sleep. Generally, young people need more sleep than older people do. Young people need about 10 to 12 hours of sleep. Very young babies may need up to 20 hours of sleep.

1. Which of the following sentences is the best conclusion for this story?
   ☐ a. Most people don't get enough sleep.
   ☐ b. Different people need different amounts of sleep.
   ☐ c. People spend about a third of their lives sleeping.

2. List details from the story to help support the conclusion you have chosen.

   ....

   ....

   ....

   ....

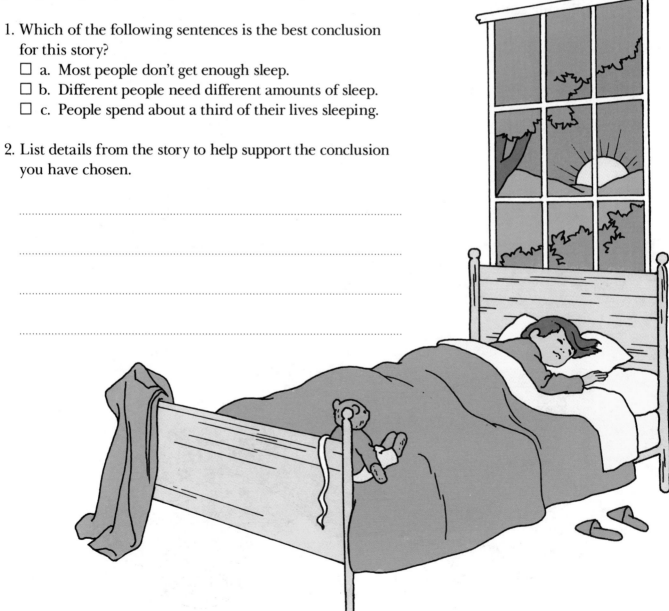

STORY 2

*E*instein was one of the smartest people who ever lived. His ideas changed the way scientists think about space and time. But Einstein could be forgetful about ordinary things. Once he attended a fancy dinner. He looked fine, except for his feet. He had forgotten to put on socks. Another time he used a check as a bookmark, even though the check was worth a large amount of money. Einstein lost the book and its valuable bookmark.

André Ampère was another brilliant scientist. Ampère made very important discoveries in math and electricity. In fact, an electrical measurement is named after him. Like Einstein, Ampère could also become so lost in thought that he would do foolish things. One night he was on his way to an important scientific meeting. While crossing a bridge, Ampère stopped to examine a strange-looking rock. Suddenly he remembered his meeting. Ampère pulled out his pocket watch and saw that he was going to be late. Ampère put the rock in his pocket, threw his watch in the river, and hurried off to the meeting.

3. Which of the following sentences is the best conclusion for this story?
   ☐ a. Electricity changed the way people live.
   ☐ b. Einstein changed the way people live.
   ☐ c. Even the smartest people sometimes do foolish things.

4. List examples from the story to help support the conclusion you have chosen.

....

....

....

....

Read the stories and answer the questions that follow.

STORY 1

*T*he March 12, 1888 weather forecast for New York City and the surrounding area predicted cloudy skies, northwesterly winds, and then clearing. The forecast was wrong. Fierce winds and heavy snows greeted New Yorkers as they arose on the morning of March 12. Snowdrifts were so high that some people had to leave their houses through the windows. The snow was piled so high that doors wouldn't open. The snow didn't stop falling until Wednesday, March 14. More than 20 inches of snow had fallen. In some places snow was piled 20 feet high. The city was paralyzed. Babies were without milk. People ran out of coal, which was used in those days to heat homes. Stores, offices, schools, and factories shut down. About 300 people died. Some had become buried in snowdrifts. Some were frozen to death in their homes. The storm's damage on land was about half a billion dollars in today's money. The damage at sea was almost as bad. Nearly 200 ships had sunk or were damaged. About 100 sailors lost their lives. New Yorkers would not soon forget the blizzard of 1888.

1. Which of the following sentences is the best conclusion for this story?
   - ☐ a. The people should have been better prepared for the blizzard.
   - ☐ b. Few blizzards occur in March.
   - ☐ c. The blizzard of 1888 did a lot of damage.

2. List details from the story to help support the conclusion you have chosen.

   ....

   ....

   ....

   ....

STORY 2

*M*any people searched for a place to stay during the blizzard. Some hotels charged five dollars for the privilege of sleeping in a chair in the lobby. One store owner sold six thousand sandwiches for five dollars each. In those days sandwiches usually cost from 10¢ to $1. Eggs were usually 25¢ a dozen. During the blizzard they cost 25¢ each. Some owners of horse-drawn buggies also charged high prices. One driver asked $50 for a ride that cost only 75¢ in fair weather.

3. Which of the following sentences is the best conclusion for this story?
   - ☐ a. Some people used the blizzard to take advantage of others.
   - ☐ b. A blizzard does strange things to people.
   - ☐ c. Many people starved to death during the blizzard.

4. List examples from the story to help support the conclusion you have chosen.

....

....

....

....

Read the stories and answer the questions that follow.

STORY 1

At the Sound School in New Haven, students study history, math, science, and English. But for science class, they board a boat. Then they sail out to sea, where they catch and study sea creatures. Students also take samples of sand from the bottom of the sea and examine the sand's contents. In English class the students read novels and short stories about the sea. In math class they learn how to plot courses between one harbor and another. The students learn to build and sail boats. The students at the Sound School have built 17 boats in the last seven years.

1. Which of the following sentences is the best conclusion for this story?
   ☐ a. The Sound School is a difficult school.
   ☐ b. Students learn about the sea at the Sound School.
   ☐ c. The Sound School is a good idea.

2. List details from the story to help support the conclusion you have chosen.

   ....

   ....

   ....

   ....

STORY 2

Would you like to groom pets for a living? There's a school that teaches students how to bathe a pet and cut its hair. First, the students practice cutting wigs. Then they try some of the simpler cuts on real dogs. Each breed of dog has a recommended style. In time, students learn to do complicated custom cuts that pet owners might request. The students also learn to handle dogs that don't behave very well and dogs whose coats are badly neglected. It takes 300 hours to complete the grooming course. In addition to working with real dogs, students must attend classes, do homework assignments, and pass a number of tests.

3. Which of the following sentences is the best conclusion for this story?
   ☐ a. It takes a lot of training to learn to groom dogs.
   ☐ b. Dog grooming is fairly easy.
   ☐ c. Small dogs are easier to groom than large dogs.

4. List details from the story to help support the conclusion you have chosen.

....

....

....

....

Read the following paragraph. Can you tell what's wrong with it?

Until a few years ago, only one company sold baseball cards. The cards were a way of getting kids to buy bubble gum. Today, there are five companies selling baseball cards. The baseball-card business is really booming.

The writer of the paragraph is trying to show that the baseball-card business is booming. The writer, however, gives just one example. The paragraph would be more convincing if the writer gave added examples. Read the following paragraph. It contains the same ideas as the first paragraph but includes more examples.

Until a few years ago, only one company sold baseball cards. The cards were a way of getting kids to buy the company's bubble gum. Today, there are five companies selling baseball cards. Fans spend twice as much money on baseball cards as they do on baseball tickets. During a recent baseball season, for example, fans spent $350 million for tickets to major league games. In that same season, they bought $750 million worth of baseball cards. Sales of baseball cards are increasing each year. For the past few years, companies have been doubling the number of cards they print. The number of people selling baseball cards has also greatly increased. Just five years ago, there were only a few stores and dealers selling baseball cards. Today, there are more than 10,000 dealers and more than 3,500 stores selling baseball cards. Fans can't seem to get enough baseball cards. The baseball-card business is booming.

In the second paragraph the author gives a number of facts to show that the baseball-card business is booming. Because the author has given more facts to support his or her conclusion, there's a better chance that you will agree with the author.

Read the following selection. Look for the main point the author is trying to make. See if the author has given enough examples or details so that you can agree with the author's main point. Then answer the question that follows.

A magazine issue usually begins with a meeting. The staff of the magazine meets with the managing editor. They discuss possible ideas for the stories. The managing editor decides which stories will be included in the magazine. Writers then begin gathering information for their stories. Writers may be helped by reporters. If the story is an important one, a photographer may accompany the reporter and the writer. After the story has been written, it is checked by an editor. Meanwhile, a designer plans how all the pages in the magazine will look. He or she creates a layout that shows where headlines, stories, and pictures will be put. The production staff prepares the story and pictures for printing. At last the magazine is ready for the circulation department. The circulation staff must make sure that the magazines are delivered to the right places.

Which of the following conclusions is given the most support in the selection?
- ☐ a. A managing editor has a great deal of responsibility.
- ☐ b. A lot of people help to put out a magazine.
- ☐ c. A lot of time is needed to put out a magazine.

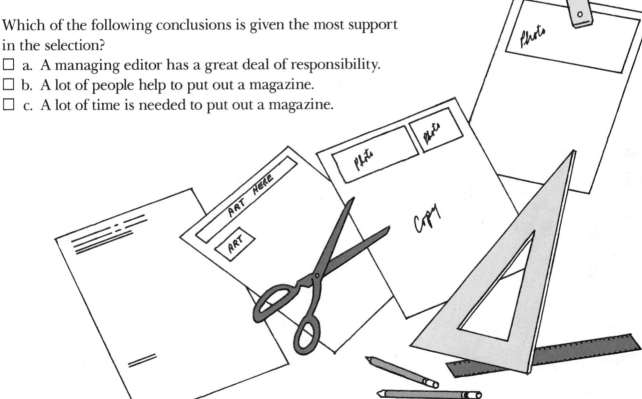

Read the stories and answer the questions.

STORY 1

Bloodhounds are often trained as search-and-rescue dogs
because of their keen sense of smell. The dogs must also be
good learners. They have to go through many hours of special
training. The dogs need to be strong. During their search, they
may have to climb steep mountains or push their way through
swampy fields. Bloodhounds have to be able to concentrate. A
bloodhound wouldn't be very useful if it chased a rabbit in the
middle of a search.

Which of the following conclusions is given the most support
in the story?

☐ a. Most dogs cannot be used for searches because they
are too easily distracted.

☐ b. Training a bloodhound to be a search-and-rescue dog
is costly.

☐ c. Bloodhounds trained to be search-and-rescue dogs
need several special qualities.

STORY 2

Marilyn Greene wanted to be a state trooper but she was
turned down. Disappointed, she joined a group that searched
for lost people. Greene quickly learned the habits of those
people who were lost in the wilderness. She discovered, for
example, that older people head for lower ground and that
hunters follow streams. Greene used her knowledge to find lost
people when others had given up the search. In 1979 she
started a business to locate lost people. Greene uses trained
dogs and special equipment, but she also uses common sense.
Once she located a man who had disappeared 20 years before.
She found out where he was in just 20 minutes by making three
phone calls.

Which of the following conclusions is given the most support
in this story?

☐ a. Greene would have made an outstanding state
trooper.

☐ b. Greene is good at finding people.

☐ c. Greene handles search-and-rescue dogs very well.

Read the stories and answer the questions.

STORY 1

Until the early 1500s, French kings wore their hair long, as did the people of France. But in 1521 a royal snowball battle led to the return of short hair. One wintry evening, King Francis I gathered some knights and attacked a friend's house with snowballs. Francis's kingly head was accidentally hit with a lighted torch. In order to treat the king's badly burned scalp, it was necessary to shave his head. By the time the king had recovered from his burns, some of his hair had grown back. Of course, his hair was not nearly as long as it had been. When they saw the king's short hair, the men of France decided that it was a new fashion.

When Louis XIII, another French king, was on the throne, beards were in style. Unfortunately, Louis could only sprout a few scraggly whiskers. Perhaps because he was disappointed with his beard, the king ordered many of the men who lived at the palace to shave. The men of France quickly took the hint. Beards started to disappear fast.

Which of the following conclusions is given the most support in the story?
☐ a. There were once many strange customs.
☐ b. People followed the king's lead in hairstyles.
☐ c. Rulers were often cruel.

STORY 2

Margaret Knight got an early start in the field of inventing. When she was just 12 years old, Knight saw a flying piece of metal from a machine injure a man. Knight created a device that would stop the machine if a piece of metal came loose from its holder. Knight's most important invention was developed 20 years later. Knight devised a machine that folded strips of paper into paper bags. Over the years, Knight invented a better window, a machine that helped to make shoes, and a number of parts for cars.

Which of the following conclusions is given the most support in the story?
☐ a. Knight's invention made the paper bag popular.
☐ b. Knight became very rich.
☐ c. Knight invented a number of useful devices.

Read the following questions and write your answers on the lines.

1. What is a conclusion?

....

....

2. How do you draw a conclusion?

....

....

3. In a magazine article, a newspaper article, or a book, find a conclusion that is supported by at least three facts or examples. Write the conclusion and its supporting details below.

Conclusion

....

....

Supporting Details

a. ....

....

b. ....

....

c. ....

....

Read the following selection. As you read, think about the conclusion you might draw from the details given. Then see if you can locate the fact that doesn't belong because it doesn't support the conclusion.

Are the walls of your classroom yellow or blue? In a school in Canada, white, beige, and brown walls were painted blue or yellow. Some students' scores on a test of thinking improved. Attendance also improved. Yellow and blue are good colors for a dentist's or doctor's office. Shades of blue make people less fearful. Gray, silver, and black are popular colors for new cars. On the other hand, red and orange make the blood flow faster and the heart beat more quickly.

The selection states that some colors help students to do better in school, some colors calm people, others excite people, and some help people to feel more trusting. From those details, you can conclude that colors affect the way people feel and act. The sentence that tells about car colors, "Gray, silver, and black are popular colors for new cars," doesn't really explain how colors affect people. A detail that doesn't help support a conclusion is unrelated.

The writer could give more details to support the selection's conclusion.

Which of the following details helps to prove the selection's conclusion?
- ☐ a. Purple is known as a royal color because kings and queens wear purple.
- ☐ b. Pink rooms help angry people calm down.
- ☐ c. Businesspeople prefer blue or gray rather than brown clothing.

The only detail that helps to prove the conclusion is *b,* which tells you that the color pink calms people down. Details *a* and *c* give additional information about colors certain people wear. But that information doesn't tell how colors affect people's feelings or actions.

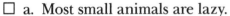

Exercise A

Read the story and answer the questions that follow.

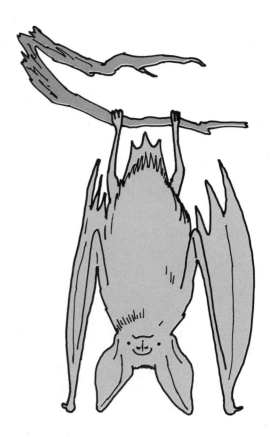

Some animals spend most of their days and nights sleeping. Bats and cats may sleep 20 out of 24 hours. Possums and porcupines sleep about 18 hours a day. On the other hand, mice only sleep about 13 hours a day. Some large animals sleep even less than that. Horses, cows, and elephants sleep only 3 or 4 hours a day. Leopards sleep on tree branches.

Which of the following sentences is the best conclusion for this story?
☐ a. Most small animals are lazy.
☐ b. Animals need different amounts of sleep.
☐ c. Animals sleep in quiet places.

Which of the following details helps to support the conclusion you have chosen?
☐ a. Some animals dream while they sleep.
☐ b. A fox digs up the ground before going to sleep.
☐ c. A mole sleeps about 8 or 9 hours each day.

Which of the following details does <u>not</u> support the conclusion you have chosen?
☐ a. Leopards sleep on tree branches.
☐ b. Bats and cats may sleep 20 out of 24 hours.
☐ c. Possums and porcupines sleep about 18 hours a day.

Exercise B

Read the stories and answer the questions.

STORY 1

*A*bout 10 years ago Lynne Frank and her husband John
started a center for hurt or sick birds. Now, scientists from a
large company help them clean up birds who have oil on their
feathers. Seven vets from animal hospitals help out on their
days off. A nearby hospital gives the center bandages and
other supplies. Summer is the busiest time at the center.
Because of all the assistance it's getting, the center is able to
take care of more than a thousand birds each year.

1. Which of the following sentences is the best conclusion
   for this story?
   ☐ a. A number of people and groups help the bird center.
   ☐ b. Little is known about the care of wild birds.
   ☐ c. The center has grown over the years.

2. Which of the following details helps to support the
   conclusion you have chosen?
   ☐ a. The people at the center are learning about birds.
   ☐ b. Oil companies give the center thousands of dollars
        each year.
   ☐ c. Many birds are dying from poisons put on lawns
        and trees.

3. Which of the following details does <u>not</u> support the
   conclusion you have chosen?
   ☐ a. Summer is the busiest time at the center.
   ☐ b. Vets from animal hospitals help out on their
        days off.
   ☐ c. A nearby hospital gives the center bandages
        and other supplies.

In 1909 Alice Ramsey and three companions set out to drive across the United States. Roads were poor in those days, and cars weren't as well built or reliable as they are today. Only about 20 men had ever been able to drive across the country. Ramsey drove over poor roads and through storms. She had no problem handling the car. Once she repaired a broken part of the car with wire. After 59 days, Ramsey finally reached San Francisco.

Ramsey continued to drive until she was in her 90s. She crossed the United States more than 30 times. Her husband was a lawmaker. In all those years, she was never in an accident—not even a minor one.

4. Which of the following sentences is the best conclusion for this story?
   ☐ a. Ramsey was a good driver and knew a lot about cars.
   ☐ b. Ramsey came from a very rich family.
   ☐ c. Ramsey made many friends over the years.

5. Which of the following details helps to support the conclusion you have chosen?
   ☐ a. When the car's motor broke, Ramsey fixed it.
   ☐ b. Cars were cheaper in 1909.
   ☐ c. The best roads were in the eastern part of the United States.

6. Which of the following details does not support the conclusion you have chosen?
   ☐ a. Once Ramsey fixed a broken part of the car with wire.
   ☐ b. Ramsey was never in an accident.
   ☐ c. Ramsey's husband was a lawmaker.

Read the stories and answer the questions that follow.

STORY 1

*T*he first wheelbarrow was made more than 2,000 years ago in China. Wheelbarrows weren't used in other countries until about 700 years ago. The Chinese also invented paper and paper money. Umbrellas, fishing reels, rockets, kites, and the iron plow were first made in China. China has more people than any other country on Earth.

1. Which of the following sentences is the best conclusion for this story?
   - ☐ a. China was the home of a number of important inventions.
   - ☐ b. China is a distant land.
   - ☐ c. China was closed to visitors for many years.

2. Which of the following details helps to support the conclusion you have chosen?
   - ☐ a. Wheelbarrows are still in use today.
   - ☐ b. Rice is one of China's main foods.
   - ☐ c. Matches were invented by the Chinese about 1,400 years ago.

3. Which of the following details does <u>not</u> support the conclusion you have chosen?
   - ☐ a. China has more people than any other country on Earth.
   - ☐ b. The first wheelbarrow was made more than 2,000 years ago in China.
   - ☐ c. The Chinese invented paper and paper money.

STORY 2

As a boy, Henry Cisneros built model airplanes. He also played the piano. Somehow, Henry found the time to read. One summer he read 50 books. Henry also liked to write. He wrote a number of poems and stories. While he was still in school, one of his poems was printed in a book. As an adult, Henry became the mayor of San Antonio, Texas.

4. What is the best conclusion for this story?
   ☐ a. As a boy, Henry had many different interests.
   ☐ b. Henry was good at most sports.
   ☐ c. Henry had trouble in school.

5. Which of the following details helps to support the story's conclusion?
   ☐ a. Henry's grandfather came to the United States from Mexico in 1926.
   ☐ b. Henry has two daughters.
   ☐ c. Henry played the French horn in the school band.

6. Which of the following details does not support the story's conclusion?
   ☐ a. As a boy, Henry built model airplanes.
   ☐ b. Somehow Henry found time to read.
   ☐ c. As an adult, Henry became mayor of San Antonio, Texas.

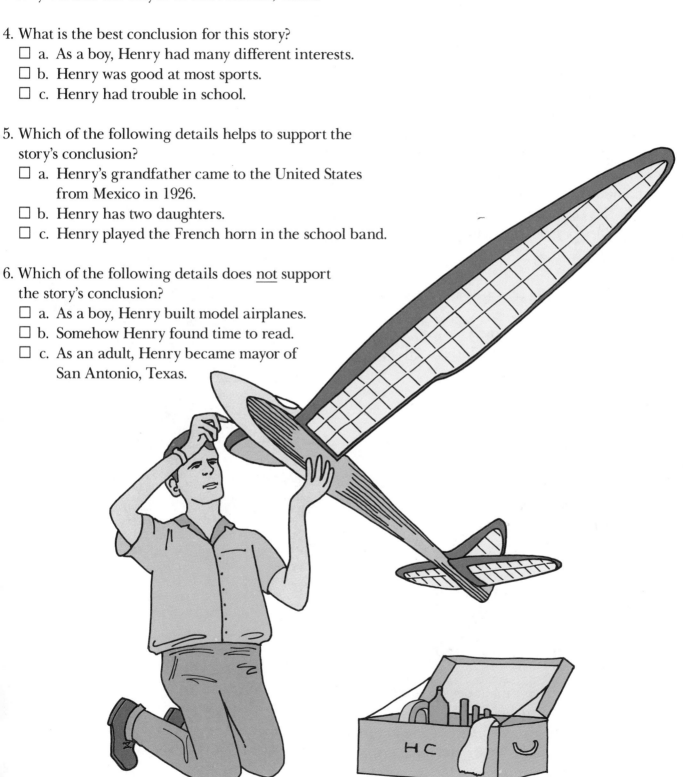

Read the following stories and answer the questions.

STORY 1

Nancy Wang was blinded by a head injury. How could she use a computer? With a special attachment, and the right kind of programs, a computer can make speech sounds. Wang can hear what she types. Computers sometimes have Braille printers so that blind people can read what they've typed. Braille writing was invented by Louis Braille while he was still a student. For people who can see a little, there are computers whose screens make letters and numbers larger. For people who can't use their arms or hands, there are a number of other ways to type on a computer. One of the simplest ways is to use a pointer that is attached to a headband. The person strikes keys with the pointer. A person can run a computer by moving a knee or elbow, blinking an eye, or blowing into a straw.

1. Which of the following sentences is the best conclusion for this story?
   □ a. Computers are useful tools for the disabled.
   □ b. Changing a computer to fit the needs of the disabled can be costly.
   □ c. Computers can be changed so that disabled people can use them.

2. Which of the following details helps to support the story's conclusion?
   □ a. There are special keyboards and software for those people who can't hold down two keys at the same time.
   □ b. Personal computers are cheaper and more powerful than they used to be.
   □ c. Several million computers are in use in schools in the United States and Canada.

3. Which of the following details does <u>not</u> support the story's conclusion?
   □ a. One of the simplest input devices is a pointer that is attached to a headband.
   □ b. For people who can see a little, there are computers whose screens make letters and numbers larger.
   □ c. Braille writing was invented by Louis Braille while he was still a student.

STORY 2

Scientists wanted to find out what happened when chickens were given special treatment. Chicken was once an expensive meat and was eaten only on special occasions. The scientists spoke kind words to the chickens in Group A. The scientists also sang soothing songs to them and gently patted their feathers. Chickens in Group B were ignored. Those in Group C were yelled at. All the chickens were given exactly the same amount of food. The chickens in Group A, however, gained more weight. They didn't get sick as often. The chickens in Group A were also friendlier than the chickens in the other two groups.

4. Which of the following sentences is the best conclusion for this story?
   ☐ a. Raising chickens is not as easy as it seems.
   ☐ b. Chickens that are treated kindly grow to be healthier and fatter.
   ☐ c. Unless they are given proper care, chickens are likely to become sick.

5. Which of the following details helps to support the story's conclusion?
   ☐ a. Many chickens are raised in huge factory-like barns and never see daylight.
   ☐ b. Chickens in Group A recovered from illness more quickly than chickens in Groups B and C did.
   ☐ c. There are nearly 200 varieties of chickens.

6. Which of the following details does not support the story's conclusion?
   ☐ a. The chickens in Group A gained more weight.
   ☐ b. The chickens in Group A were also friendlier.
   ☐ c. Chicken was once an expensive meat and was eaten only on special occasions.

2

Detecting Unrelated Facts

You and your friend are discussing the question: Which dog makes the best pet? Your friend says that collies make the best pets. Your friend gives the following reasons. In those reasons see if you can find any details or reasons that are unrelated. An unrelated detail or reason is one that doesn't explain in some way why collies make the best pets.

Collies make the best pets. Collies are loyal and friendly. They enjoy people and will greet you with a lively wag of the tail when you return. We have a collie and so do our neighbors up the street. Collies are smart and easy to train. Collies were originally raised in Scotland to herd sheep. The most famous collie is Lassie who appeared in several movies and on TV.

Did you locate the details that are unrelated? There are several. The fact that your friend and her neighbor have collies doesn't mean that they are good pets. The fact that collies were originally raised in Scotland to herd sheep doesn't mean that collies make good pets either. The final unrelated fact is in the last sentence. The fact that Lassie is the most famous collie does not help you decide that collies make good pets.

Unrelated details often appear in discussions, arguments, and advertisements. They even appear in books, newspapers, and magazines. It's important to know that a detail is unrelated. Sometimes people are persuaded by unrelated details. When you draw a conclusion or make a decision, you should pay attention only to details that are related.

Read the following paragraphs. Each paragraph has one unrelated detail. Find the main point or message of each paragraph. Then look for any detail that doesn't support that main point or message. Underline the unrelated detail once you have found it.

1. Frank Tatterone, the new first baseman, is not very good. Yesterday he struck out three times and made two errors. Besides, he never gives autographs.

2. Crunchy Munchies are loaded with vitamins and minerals. Singing star Melissa Vanderson starts each day with a giant bowl of Crunchy Munchies. When eaten with milk, Crunchy Munchies supply one-third of the body's necessary vitamins and minerals.

3. The greatest slugger of all time was Babe Ruth. In the 1927 season, he set a record by hitting 60 home runs. During his playing days, he hit 714 home runs, a record that has only been broken once. Babe Ruth was a generous man and often visited children in hospitals.

4. Carmen should be president of the stamp club. She's been collecting stamps for five years. She's read several books about stamps. She's lived in this town all her life. She has been the president of two other clubs and knows how to run meetings.

5. Carl is my choice for the lead part in the play. He's been in three plays. He goes to acting classes on Saturdays. And he's my best friend.

Read the following questions and write your answers on the lines.

1. What is the difference between a related and an unrelated detail?

   ....

   ....

2. In a library book, newspaper, magazine, or school book, locate at least two paragraphs or passages that contain one or more unrelated details. Write the conclusion of each passage and the detail that is unrelated.

   Passage 1:

   Conclusion ....

   ....

   Unrelated Detail ....

   ....

   Passage 2:

   Conclusion ....

   ....

   Unrelated Detail ....

   ....

Sources of Information

You want to find out if the sun is a good source of energy for the future. That's a difficult question. You need to ask an expert. An expert has usually studied and worked in his or her field for many years. He or she may also have written some books and magazine articles. An expert on solar energy may be a person who teaches about energy at a college. He or she may be someone who helps the government solve energy problems. Or an expert could be someone who owns a company that gives advice about energy.

To get expert information, you can write or talk to the person. You can also read what the person has written in a book or magazine article.

To get information you can really trust, however, you need more than just an expert. You need an expert who has nothing to lose or gain by giving information. For example, if you get information from an expert who works for an oil company, the expert might favor oil as the best source of energy. Because the expert works for an oil company, he or she may not want to recommend coal or sun power because that might make his or her boss angry.

Be careful that the expert is not talking about areas in which he or she has no special knowledge. For example, a person who is an expert baseball player may recommend certain foods. If you want expert knowledge about foods, you should get it from a food scientist, not a baseball player.

Look at the information given about the following people. First, decide if the person is an expert. If the person is an expert, write **E** on the line. Next, decide whether the person can be completely fair. In other words, he or she should give information that is based only on the facts. Put **F** on the line also if you think the person will be fair. If the person is not an expert, do not write on the line.

.... 1. Alice Langley is called the "energy doctor." When big companies or the government have questions about energy, they ask Langley. Langley owns a company that gives advice about energy. She has written a book about the advantages and disadvantages of the main kinds of energy.

.... 2. Sam London never went to college, but he has read a dozen books and nearly a hundred articles about solar energy. Sam owns a company that builds homes and factories that use solar power.

.... 3. Professor Ruth Avery teaches about solar energy at the state's largest college. She has also written a book about solar energy and is carrying out experiments using solar power.

.... 4. Anita Lopez is vice-president of the city's natural gas company. Before working for the gas company, she studied solar power in college and wrote three books about solar power.

.... 5. Ralph Jackson has been interested in solar power for nearly two years. He's read three books on the subject and has had a solar hot water heater put in his home.

Read the following passages and then answer the questions about getting information from the best sources. Remember that the best sources of information will be experts who are fair.

1. You want to know what your baseball card collection is worth. Where would you be likely to get the best information?
   - ☐ a. a new book about baseball cards written by two men who have been collecting cards for 20 years
   - ☐ b. the owner of a baseball card store who wants to buy your collection
   - ☐ c. your older brother, who collected cards when he was your age

2. You are raising a pig as a 4-H project. Your pig seems tired all the time and isn't eating its food. You wonder what's wrong with the pig. Who would be most likely to give you the best information?
   - ☐ a. your cousin, who is also raising a pig
   - ☐ b. a veterinarian
   - ☐ c. a farmer who has some chickens and pigs but mostly raises wheat

3. You are having trouble with your spelling. You study your words, but you still get low marks on your weekly tests. Who would be best able to help you?
   - ☐ a. your teacher
   - ☐ b. the student who is the best speller in the class
   - ☐ c. your older sister who also has trouble with spelling

4. You're the pitcher for your Little League team. The league championship begins the day after tomorrow. Your arm has been sore for more than a week. You wonder if you should stop pitching for a while. Who would be most likely to give you the best advice?
   - ☐ a. the coach of your team
   - ☐ b. the gym teacher
   - ☐ c. your family doctor

5. You have just started playing tennis and you wonder which racquet is best for you. Who would be most likely to give you the best information?
   - ☐ a. the owner of a sports shop
   - ☐ b. a teacher who plays tennis
   - ☐ c. the coach of a young person's tennis team

Read the stories and answer the questions.

STORY 1

*W*hen she was just 12 years old, Charlayne Hunter-Gault decided that she wanted to be a news reporter. Her grandmother may have had something to do with her decision. Although her grandmother had only gone to school through the third grade, she read three newspapers a day. In college Charlayne Hunter-Gault studied newspaper and TV reporting. Since her graduation from college, she has worked for *The New York Times*, one of the country's best newspapers. She has also worked for several magazines and a number of TV stations. Since 1978, she has been a reporter on a national news program. Over the years, she has received dozens of awards for her stories.

Charlayne Hunter-Gault would give the best information about
☐ a. what makes a good grandmother.
☐ b. the importance of hard work.
☐ c. gathering information for a news story.

STORY 2

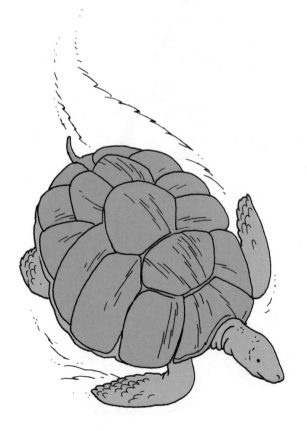

*A*s a boy, Archie Carr collected turtles and frogs. As an adult scientist, he became interested in green sea turtles. He had a theory that green sea turtles swam from an island in the Atlantic to South America. That is a 1,200-mile swim. Carr believed that the turtles did it twice. After their first swim, they swam back to the island to lay their eggs. Two such long swims seemed impossible. Some people wondered how the turtles could swim that far. Others wondered how they could find their way. Carr wanted to prove his theory. He put tags on the turtles. With the help of the tags, he proved that the turtles did make two long swims.

During his studies, Dr. Carr discovered that trash in the ocean is harming giant turtles. Giant turtles will bite at anything. Sometimes they snap at bits of tar made from spilled oil. The tar glues their jaws shut. Then the turtles can't eat and many of them die. Archie Carr wrote a number of articles and several books about turtles before he died in 1987. During much of his life, he was known as the "turtle man."

Archie Carr would give the best information about the
☐ a. best ways to get rid of ocean trash.
☐ b. world's endangered animals.
☐ c. ways of giant turtles.

Read the stories and answer the questions.

STORY 1

*R*oberta Henry has spent many years studying about foods that are best for the body. She is in charge of planning meals at Children's Hospital in Boston. Henry knows that some foods actually speed healing. Roberta Henry is the co-author of a book about foods.

Roberta Henry would give the best information about
- ☐ a. why people don't like certain foods.
- ☐ b. how to plan tasty meals when you don't have much money.
- ☐ c. healthful foods.

STORY 2

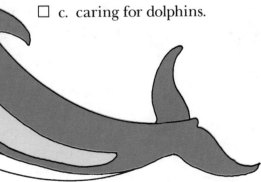

*I*n 1960 Sam Ridgway became a veterinarian. In 1962 Dr. Ridgway was the vet at an Air Force base. He looked after pets and the base's guard dogs. He was asked by the United States Navy to become a vet on a project in which dolphins were studied and trained. From 1962 to 1987, Dr. Ridgway worked with all sorts of dolphins. During that time, he went back to school for two years to learn more about how sea creatures' brains and nerves work. Dr. Ridgway gave talks all over the world about dolphins, wrote articles about dolphins, and wrote a book about Tuffy, one of the Navy's best-trained dolphins.

Dr. Ridgway would give the best information about
- ☐ a. choosing a pet.
- ☐ b. life at sea.
- ☐ c. caring for dolphins.

Read the stories and answer the questions.

STORY 1

Do you want your tapes to last longer and sound better? Then take care of them. First, keep them in their plastic boxes. This protects them from dust. Also keep your tapes away from heat. Sunlight or heat from radiators can warp your cassettes. Make sure that you keep your tapes out of the rain and away from other kinds of moisture. Magnetic fields can harm your tapes, too. Telephones and motors have magnetic fields. Don't touch the tape with your fingers. Body oils can harm tapes. Make sure your tapes are wound up tightly before you play them. You can do this by turning one of the little wheels in the center of the tape with a pencil point.

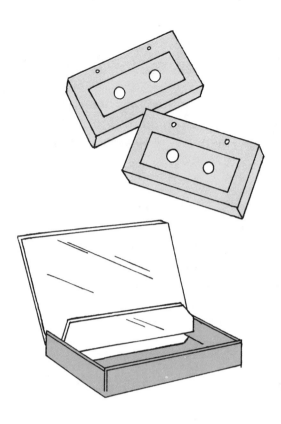

You would probably believe the information given in the story if the information came from a

☐ a. company that makes tapes.

☐ b. teacher at school.

☐ c. neighbor who just got a new tape player.

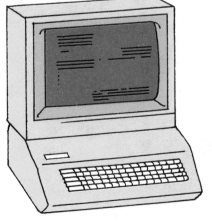

STORY 2

Typing is an important skill. In high school and college, students are sometimes asked to type their assignments. Typing can also lead to a good job. Businesses always need typists. Typing is important if you plan to work with computers. In order to be able to run a computer, you have to press keys similar to the keys on a typewriter. If you're a slow typist or make a lot of mistakes, you may have difficulty using a computer. Computers are found in millions of homes, schools, and offices. In the future, they'll be found in many more places. At some time or another, most people will find themselves running a computer. Typing, which is sometimes known as keyboarding, will become almost as important as writing.

You would probably believe the information in this story if it came from

☐ a. a typing teacher.

☐ b. the inventor of a newer, more powerful computer.

☐ c. a scientist who studies the future.

Read the stories and answer the questions.

STORY 1

*M*any people eat too much fat. Fat is found in hamburgers, steaks, and other red meats. Fat is also found in butter, cheese, and whole milk. Potato chips are loaded with fat, as are French fries and cheese puffs. To cut down on fat, eat fewer fried foods. Two or three times a week, eat chicken, turkey, or fish instead of meat. Eat baked potatoes rather than French fries, but don't smother them with butter. Drink low-fat milk instead of whole milk and use soft margarine instead of butter. The body needs some fat to stay healthy. But too much fat might shorten your life.

You would probably believe the information in this story if it came from
☐ a. the author of a cookbook.
☐ b. a food scientist.
☐ c. the owner of a health-food restaurant.

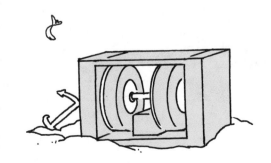

STORY 2

*I*n the future, more of our power will come from the sea. The tides and waves will be used to run machines that make electricity. The Gulf Stream will also be used for power. The Gulf Stream is a swiftly moving current of warm water that flows in the Atlantic Ocean. The Gulf Stream's strong currents will be used to turn turbines, which are machines that generate electricity. The turbines will be about 500 feet in diameter and will be 75 feet below the surface of the sea so that ships can pass over them. Giant anchors will keep the turbines in place.

You would probably believe the information in this story if it came from
☐ a. a sea captain.
☐ b. a city planner.
☐ c. an energy scientist.

Read the following questions and write your answers on the lines.

1. What are the main qualities you should look for in a source of information?

    ....

    ....

2. In your school or town library, locate three nonfiction books. Try to get books that are up-to-date. Read the back cover of each book to get information about the author. Write the author's name and the title of the book. Tell why you think the author is or is not a good source of information.

    a. Author ....

        Title ....

        Rate the source of information: ....

        ....

        ....

    b. Author ....

        Title ....

        Rate the source of information: ....

        ....

        ....

    c. Author ....

        Title ....

        Rate the source of information: ....

        ....

        ....

1

Methods That Persuade

Propaganda (prop uh GAN duh) is the use of words or symbols to persuade you to believe an idea, buy a product, or take some other action. Propaganda appeals to your feelings instead of to your mind.

For example, you are watching an ad on TV. Your favorite star is talking about Juice, a new soft drink that's supposed to taste like orange juice, only better. In your mind, you associate the star with the soft drink. When you see Juice in the store, you think of that star and buy the soft drink.

Advertisers often use propaganda. People who are running for mayor or president use propaganda. Propaganda can be used for good causes as well as bad causes. Propaganda can be used to persuade people to exercise more often, which is healthy. But it can also be used to get them to eat products that contain too much fat, salt, or sugar.

There are several common methods of propaganda. Here are some of the ones that are frequently used.

Testimonial. Testimonial is the method that was used to sell Juice. A singer, actor, athlete, or other well-known person gives a testimonial for a product or idea. That is, the person speaks in favor of it. There are two things wrong with testimonials. First, a singer is not an expert about soft drinks. Second, even if the singer were an expert, he or she is being paid to speak in favor of a product. The person may not say what he or she really thinks about the product. In fact, actors who have been paid to give a testimonial for one soft drink have been seen drinking other soft drinks. In many testimonials, the people simply say what they are paid to say.

Bandwagon. Bandwagon makes use of your desire to be part of a group. If everyone in your class wears a certain kind of sweater, chances are you will want one, too. People like to be part of a crowd. An ad might show dozens of teens rushing to see a new bike. You get the idea that everyone wants one of those bikes. You feel that if you buy the bike, you will be part of the crowd.

Plain Folks. Most people don't like other people who are snobs or who seem to think they are better than everyone else. Propaganda that uses the plain folks method claims that leaders or important people are really just plain, ordinary folks. A wealthy woman who is running for mayor may dress in jeans and stop for lunch at a fast-food restaurant. Other people think, "She eats at the same place I do, and she wears the same kinds of clothes that I do. She must believe in the same ideas that I do."

Card-Stacking. Card-stacking is a method that you've probably used. In card-stacking you mention all the good points of something but none of the bad points. For example, you want to join a record and tape club. You explain to your parents that you can get six records and tapes for just a dollar. You also explain that the club has the latest records and that it's convenient to order by mail. You don't mention that if you accept the introductory offer of six tapes or records for a dollar, you must buy four records or tapes at the club's regular prices. You don't say that you'll have to pay several dollars postage and handling each time you send in an order. And you don't explain that if you forget to send back the order card, the record or tape of the month is automatically sent to you even if you don't want it.

Read the following passages. Tell which method of propaganda each passage is using: bandwagon, plain folks, testimonial, or card-stacking.

.... 1. A candidate for president is seen fixing some broken steps on the porch of his home.

.... 2. A new bicycle is advertised as lightweight, sleek-looking, fast, and easy to pedal. The ad doesn't say that the bike costs more than similar bikes, has a frame that is easily bent, and needs frequent repairs.

.... 3. Randolph Felton, a star pitcher, says that an Action camera is his choice when taking sports photos. "Action captures the action every time," Felton promises.

.... 4. *Mystery at Midnight* is advertised as the thriller that you can't put down. "Everybody's reading it," the ad says.

.... 5. The governor plays basketball with some teenagers in a city playground.

.... 6. Ralph Fletcher, who plays a doctor in a television series, advertises a new pain reliever. He says the new pain reliever gets rid of his headaches fast.

.... 7. The governor is running for reelection. She tells the voters that she has lowered taxes and that there are more jobs in the state than ever. The governor doesn't say that because of the lower taxes no new roads or hospitals will be built and that several state buildings have to put off repairs because there is not enough money.

.... 8. In a TV ad a group of runners is cheering for Speedos, the sneakers that make you feel like running.

.... 9. The ad for CD players explains that the sound is terrific and that compact discs last for a long time. The ad doesn't say that compact discs cost more than tapes or records and may be ruined if they are scratched.

.... 10. In a magazine ad Angela Lopez, a tennis star, says that in between matches she eats Crunchies. "Crunchies give you quick energy," she announces.

2

More Methods That Persuade

Below are three more methods of propaganda. As you read about the methods, try to think of a time when you may have seen them used.

Transfer. In transfer a well-known and well-liked symbol or person is presented along with a product, idea, or another person. The purpose of the method is to have people transfer the good feeling that they have for the person or symbol to another product, idea, or person. For example, a car company uses an eagle in its ads. When people in the United States see an eagle, they think of an animal that is strong and free. They also think of the United States, since the eagle is the country's national bird. The car maker hopes that people transfer all those feelings to its car.

Name-calling. Name-calling gives people a bad feeling about a person, object, or idea. The unpleasant name creates anger, fear, or disgust in the reader or listener. A person running for office might call the person he or she is running against a "bully." People don't like bullies, so they dislike the person who is called a bully. A candidate might say that his rival "has a bunch of old ideas." Voters dislike the ideas because they are old. They don't even think about what the ideas are. Name-calling convinces people to make decisions without carefully thinking about the person, idea, or object in question.

Glittering Generalities. This method is sometimes called glad names. In an ad a product might be described as *wonderful* or *great.* No attempt is made to prove why the product is so wonderful or so great. The ad tries to convince people by using special words. The ad or article might also use scientific words. The ad might say that the toothpaste has *sodium chloride.* Sodium chloride sounds important. People think that the toothpaste will be really good. Sodium chloride, however, is just salt.

Read the following passages. Tell which method of propaganda each passage is using: transfer, name-calling, or glittering generalities.

.... 1. Frank's Clothing Stores. A name you can trust. We offer the finest in high-quality clothing. Shop at Frank's and look your best.

.... 2. George Perkins is running for mayor and gives a speech on television. Perkins is seated at a large desk. On his desk is a picture of his family. Behind him is a large United States flag.

.... 3. The sleek new Fasttrack is a dream car. It has room for six passengers and lots of packages, but it handles like a sportscar. It's a fun car to drive. Take a look at the great new Fasttrack. Better yet, test drive this wonderful machine.

.... 4. Oak City badly needs a new stadium. Oak Field is an ugly, uncomfortable ballpark that should have been replaced years ago. Oak Field has only 10,000 seats. That might have been enough seats 50 years ago when Oak City had only 20,000 people. But Oak City has grown. Today, nearly 50,000 people make their home in or around Oak City. It's time we replaced that cramped eyesore with a park that meets the needs of today's citizens.

.... 5. Shop at Winston's Food Stores. Super service. Outstanding selection of delicious farm-fresh fruits and vegetables. Excellent selection of time-saving frozen dinners.

.... 6. Get rid of dog odors, stale cigarette and cigar smoke, cooking smells, and other embarrassing odors. Use Clean Air to freshen your home.

Unit Eight Review

Read the following questions and write your answers on the lines.

1. What is propaganda?

....

....

....

2. What are the names of seven propaganda devices? Briefly explain how each one works.

a. ....

....

....

b. ....

....

....

c. ....

....

....

d. ....

....

....

e. ....

....

....

f. ....

....

....

g. ....

....

....

3. From radio, TV, newspapers, magazines, or speeches, find one example of each of the seven types of propaganda.

Type of Propaganda Device   Example

a. ....

    ....

b. ....

    ....

c. ....

    ....

d. ....

    ....

e. ....

    ....

f. ....

    ....

g. ....

    ....

Learning to Read & Think Scope & Sequence

Facts and Opinions	Distinguishing between facts and opinions
	Identifying words that signal opinion statements
	Verifying factual statements
	Recognizing analytical statements
	Applying the concept of facts and opinions
How Words Are Used	Identifying the uses of words
	Recognizing words that have favorable connotations
	Recognizing words that have unfavorable connotations
	Identifying persuasive language
	Applying the concept of the uses of words
Unfair Writing/Slanted Writing	Recognizing slanted writing
	Recognizing fair writing
	Identifying judgmental words in slanted writing
	Applying the concept of slanted writing
	Recognizing biased writing
	Applying the concept of biased writing
	Recognizing assumptions in writing
	Applying the concept of assumptions in writing
Author's Purpose	Identifying the author's purpose
	Recognizing the author's purpose
	Contrasting the author's purpose
	Applying the concept of the author's purpose
Conclusions	Recognizing logical conclusions
	Supporting logical conclusions
	Judging sufficiency of support for a conclusion
	Applying the concept of logical, sufficiently supported conclusions
Related and Unrelated Details	Recognizing unrelated details
	Recognizing related details
	Detecting unrelated details in persuasive language
	Applying the concept of related and unrelated details
Judging Sources	Judging the competence and the fairness of a source of information
	Recognizing the best source of information
	Judging recency of written source of information
	Evaluating sources of information
	Applying the concept of competence and fairness of sources of information
Propaganda	Identifying four major methods of propaganda
	Identifying seven major methods of propaganda
	Applying the concept of detecting propaganda methods
	Identifying common fallacies in reasoning
	Applying the concept of fallacies

Book B/C	Book D	Book E	Book F	Book G	Book H
✓	✓	✓	✓	✓	✓
✓	✓	✓	✓	✓	✓
✓	✓	✓	✓	✓	✓
		✓	✓	✓	✓
✓	✓	✓	✓	✓	✓
✓	✓	✓	✓	✓	✓
✓	✓	✓	✓	✓	✓
✓	✓	✓	✓	✓	✓
✓	✓	✓	✓	✓	✓
✓	✓	✓	✓	✓	✓
✓	✓	✓	✓	✓	✓
✓	✓	✓	✓	✓	✓
✓	✓	✓	✓	✓	✓
✓	✓	✓	✓	✓	✓
				✓	✓
				✓	✓
				✓	✓
				✓	✓
✓	✓	✓	✓	✓	✓
✓	✓	✓	✓	✓	✓
✓	✓	✓	✓	✓	✓
✓	✓	✓	✓	✓	✓
✓	✓	✓	✓	✓	✓
✓	✓	✓	✓	✓	✓
✓	✓	✓	✓	✓	✓
✓	✓	✓	✓	✓	✓
✓	✓	✓	✓	✓	✓
✓	✓	✓	✓	✓	✓
		✓	✓	✓	✓
✓	✓	✓	✓	✓	✓
✓	✓	✓	✓	✓	✓
✓	✓	✓	✓	✓	✓
				✓	✓
				✓	✓
✓	✓	✓	✓	✓	✓
		✓			
			✓	✓	✓
		✓	✓	✓	✓
				✓	✓
				✓	✓

About the Author

Dr. Gunning is a professor in the Reading Department at Southern Connecticut State University, where he teaches graduate methods courses in reading and language arts. He has been an elementary school reading consultant, junior high reading specialist and English teacher, English department head, and senior high school English teacher.

Dr. Gunning has written four books for young people: *Dream Cars, Unexplained Mysteries, Amazing Escapes,* and *Strange Mysteries.* The latter three titles have been recommended by the American Library Association's High/Low Committee for use with older reluctant readers. Dr. Gunning is also an author for two reading series for older, disabled readers, comprehension materials, and a method text, *Teaching Phonics and Other Word Attack Skills.*

Dr. Gunning is a past president of the Connecticut Association for Reading Research, membership chairman of the Readability Special Interest Group, and a member of the International Reading Association, New England Reading Association, and National Council of Teachers of English. He is also a contributing editor for *My Friend* and a member of the panel of reading experts for *Sports Illustrated for Kids.* Dr. Gunning was recently awarded a Visiting Faculty Fellowship by Yale University to study brain development and neurological processes in reading and writing.